# Sometimes Sad Comes Out Mad

Written by Grammy Sami

For all the people
who have big feelings
that can be confusing at times,
I'm here to let you know that
you're not alone, okay?
Okay.

With Love,

*Grammy Sami*

SOMETIMES SAD COMES OUT MAD
Copyright © 2022 by Grammy Sami
Great Minds Ink, LLC

Thank you for complying with copyright laws and
thereby supporting this ever-so-grateful writer.

To contact the author:
greatmindsinkco@gmail.com
Find her on Facebook:
Grammy Sami, Children's Book Author

Written and Designed by Grammy Sami
Illustrations by Evgeniia Silaeva et al, via Canva

Grammy Sami is not a professional mental health care provider. She has
simply observed and/or experienced the things about which she writes.
Therefore, this book is presented for the purposes of encouraging
others and assuring them that they are not alone.
Grammy Sami does not diagnose, treat, or cure anyone.
She just loves BIG and wants to share that love with her readers.

ISBN 979-8-9861111-0-0 (paperback)
First Edition: April 2022

Some days are fun,
I get to run and play.
Not a care in the world,
I just laugh and laugh all day.

Other days I feel peaceful,
I relax and I rest.
The world feels good to me,
I feel so very blessed.

Me too, I have days
When I sing and I dance.
No one can bring me down.
No way, not a chance!

*Many* of my days are filled
With joy and gladness.
But then there are days
When I feel lots of sadness.

Funny thing is,
Almost no one can tell.
Because instead of crying,
I scream and I *yell*!

But when I try to find words,
I just feel at a loss.

**Why do you do this?**
**Actually, I *think* I might know.**

Feeling angry seems easier
Than feeling sad and low.

**Sharing our sadness
Can feel scary and rough.**

But acting all mad
Makes us feel pretty tough.

When I act tough,
Everyone seems to stay away.
They leave me alone,
Which I *thought* was okay.

That way I could cry
And no one would see.
But then I learned something new.
They really want to help me!

You see, it's harder to help
When someone is mad.
So I've learned to share
When I'm feeling sad.

It wasn't easy at first.
It felt a little weird,
Sharing my sad feelings
And the things that I feared.

I thought it made me weak
To cry or be scared.
But then when I did,
So many showed that they cared!

Feeling sad isn't
All that easy *or* fun.
But everyone feels it;
You're not the only one.

Of course, mad is a feeling too.
It's as real as the rain.
But I don't want to use it
To hide my true pain.

We'll always be loved,
Whether we cry or we yell.
But others can better help us
If it's the truth that we tell.

I hope you can learn
From what I've told you just now.
It's not as scary to share
Once a friend shows you how.

So go ahead,
Be sad when you're sad.

If you enjoyed reading this book, please leave an honest review on Amazon. I read every single one, and your review will help new readers discover my books.

*Thank you!!*

# About the Author

About Grammy Sami,
Oh, where should we start?
She's a grammy of three
And has a great, big heart!

She has compassion for people,
Both the young and the old.
She believes everyone's story
Should have a chance to be told.

You will soon find out
As you read her books each time
That her favorite way to write
Is with a catchy little rhyme.

Some of her books
Tackle things that are tough.
And she hopes that they'll help you
Get through some hard stuff.

Other books are lighthearted,
They are silly and fun.
You can be sure they'll rhyme,
Each and every one!

So please enjoy
As you relax and read.
And read again and again,
As many times as you need!